LITTLE BOOK OF
PERSONALITY
PSYCHOLOGY

Esther Grant

summersdale

THE LITTLE BOOK OF PERSONALITY PSYCHOLOGY

Text by Joanna Bradshaw

An Hachette UK Company
www.hachette.co.uk

Summersdale Publishers
Part of Octopus Publishing Group Limited
Carmelite House
50 Victoria Embankment
LONDON
EC4Y 0DZ
UK

www.summersdale.com

Printed and bound in Poland

ISBN: 978-1-83799-395-6

This FSC® label means
that materials used for
the product have been
responsibly sourced

MIX
Paper | Supporting
responsible forestry
FSC® C018236

Substantial discounts on bulk quantities of Summersdale books are available to corporations, professional associations and other organizations. For details contact general enquiries: telephone: +44 (0) 1243 771107 or email: enquiries@summersdale.com.

Contents

Introduction

How are you different from your friends, family and people from other cultures? How are you the same? And how did you get to be the way you are?

These are some of the questions personality psychology seeks to answer. Experts study the science of how we come to think, behave and learn, and how differences in each person's tendencies contribute to what we call their personality – a word whose roots are in the Latin word for a mask worn by stage actors: the *persona*.

We have always been fascinated by ourselves and by each other. A toddler develops the ability to recognize themselves in a mirror at around 18 months of age. This crucial point in our lives as humans sets us off on a journey to develop what's called our theory of mind: our sense that each of us is unique, with thoughts and feelings that differ from those of other people.

As humans, we naturally monitor, reflect on and judge the behaviour of others. Perhaps you've heard somebody comment that a baby is placid, good, charming, clingy or sensitive. But among personality psychologists there are fascinating debates about how much of a baby's personality is innate and how much is down to other factors like their environment, socialization and the cultural context they grow up in. Does personality predict behaviour? And can we change our personality?

In this book we'll look at how the field and theories of personality psychology developed, how personality is tested and how personality disorders are described and diagnosed. This book will give you an overview of this exciting field, equipping you with the resources to find out more about yourself too.

That said, always consult a qualified healthcare professional if you would like to get insights into your own personality, or need help if you're coping with challenges.

WHAT IS PERSONALITY PSYCHOLOGY?

From its beginnings in the philosophical inquiries of ancient Greek thinkers, personality psychology has developed as an exciting empirical field, becoming increasingly interdisciplinary. Every day brings new findings as personality psychologists work in parallel with neurobiologists, and social and behavioural psychologists in both long-established fields such as fear and aggression research, and developing ones such as functional imaging and epigenetics.

In this chapter, we'll dive into the history of personality psychology and find out why it's such a popular and useful field, not only in psychology and scientific research, but in wider culture too. Let's get started by looking at where the idea of personality came from and how early psychologists developed theories to describe it.

Humours and Temperaments

Around the end of the fifth century BCE emerged the *Hippocratic Corpus*, a collection of about 60 medical texts associated with the ancient Greek physician Hippocrates. In the Corpus was a description of four temperaments, which posited that the bodily fluids described as blood, yellow bile, black bile and phlegm were the foundations of health and disease. Prior to this, both physical and mental illness were popularly believed to have a divine cause. Hippocrates' teachings assigned four personality temperaments to a person depending on the balance of each fluid within them. Galen (CE 129–*c.*200) built on Hippocrates' teachings further in his dissertation *De temperamentis*, looking for physiological reasons for different behaviours in humans. This gave an axis of hot/cold and dry/wet on which each temperament (melancholic, choleric, sanguine and phlegmatic) could be plotted, much like the axis of neuroticism/extraversion which later personality theorists would devise. Galen's work was to remain influential for around 1,500 years, and humorism is believed to underpin East Indian Ayurvedic traditions as well as Islamic Unani medical practices.

HUMANS COTTONED ON
TO THE IDEA OF TRAITS IN
CLASSICAL TIMES... THE
SCIENTIFIC APPROACH
HAS SIMPLY CLEANED UP
THEIR NUMBER, PROVIDED
RELIABLE MEASURES,
AND VALIDATED THEM.

Ian J. Deary, *The Cambridge Handbook of Personality Psychology*

Foibles and Fads

The Greek philosopher Theophrastus (370–288 BCE) took the four temperaments further, and described in his Characters a set of sketches of "human foibles" which are not dissimilar to those type labels used in modern personality tests like 16Personalities. However, Theophrastus' versions are more colourful: "the dissembler, the flatterer, the gossip, the toady, the fop, the miser, the superstitious, the mistrusting, the querulous, the bully, the coward, the stubborn, the pompous, the boor and the bore, the malaprop, the well-intentioned fool and the public-disregarding autocrat."

These early trait descriptors were updated by Anglican clergyman John Earle in 1628 in his *Microcosmographie, or, A Peece of the World Discovered in Essayes and Characters*, and remained popular into the nineteenth century. In the meantime, scientific revolutions and foreign explorations had moved Europeans away from mysticism and religion towards an empirical description of the world, thanks to the discoveries of Galileo, Copernicus, Harvey and Darwin.

IS IT THEN POSSIBLE TO DESCRIBE ONESELF AT ONCE FAITHFULLY AND FULLY?

George Eliot, *Impressions of Theophrastus Such*

Hysterical Women

In the nineteenth century, the French neurologist Jean-Martin Charcot (1825–1893) conducted research into the phenomenon popularly referred to as "hysteria", whereby some women experienced fainting, chronic pain, seizures and loss of feeling in hands and legs. Charcot greatly influenced the ideas of Austrian physician and psychologist Sigmund Freud (1856–1939), which have become part of our everyday language (the Freudian slip, for example).

Charcort and Freud conducted experiments involving hypnosis and psychoanalytical interventions. Upon recounting often traumatic sexual experience under hypnosis, women would experience a cathartic outpouring of emotion and some improvement in their symptoms. It seemed that the symptoms were being caused not (just) by physiological but also by psychological factors, and Freud used this observation to inform his theories on the determinants of personality and behaviour.

Freud's work has had a massive impact on how we understand personality today. We'll touch on his theories later here, and *The Little Book of Psychology* (Summersdale, 2019) discusses Freud's theories and psychodynamic approach in more detail.

The Birth of the Modern Science of Personality Psychology

The early twentieth century was a time of rapid growth and interest in the field of personality psychology, although looking back, the development of various grand theories seems fragmented. Building on publications in the first decade of the 1900s by Freud, Alfred Adler, Mary Calkins and Carl Jung, in 1927 American psychologist Gordon Allport published *Concepts of Trait and Personality*. This was followed in 1937 by *Personality: A Psychological Interpretation*, the publication of which is often considered to mark the birth of the scientific field of personality research.

Back in Europe, Sigmund Freud's daughter Anna Freud was establishing herself as a psychoanalyst of children in London, after being forced to leave Austria with her father under the shadow of approaching war. Anna Freud and other notable neo-Freudians like Adler, Jung, Erik Erikson and Karen Horney modified Sigmund Freud's ideas to create new theories about personality, de-emphasizing sex and focusing more on the social environment and effects of culture on personality.

THE PRIVILEGE OF A LIFETIME IS TO BECOME WHO YOU TRULY ARE.

Carl Jung

Adventures in Typology

Carl Jung's concept of archetypes such as anima (the feminine aspect of the male psyche) and animus (the masculine aspect of the female psyche) reflected traditional gender roles and reinforced the notion of inherent psychological differences between the sexes. Jung went on to identify eight personality types, which influenced Isabel Briggs Myers' and Katharine Briggs' 1942 breakthrough in typology. The Myers-Briggs Type Indicator (MBTI) aimed to ground Jung's thinking around personality types into a quantitative assessment tool for the first time.

Most people are familiar with the MBTI, and it forms the basis of a wide range of personality tests used today in workplaces and popular culture. We'll elaborate on this and other personality tests in chapter three.

Psychoanalytic and behavioural models of personality were complemented during the 1950s and 1960s by the theories of humanistic psychologists, including Abraham Maslow and Carl Rogers, social cognitive theories and biological theories.

How Does Understanding Your Personality Help You?

Acknowledging and being curious about the personalities of your loved ones can help you establish better, more empathetic relationships driven by understanding and curiosity.

Awareness of your own personality traits can help you develop in a direction that naturally suits your strengths and temperament and help you identify values that are important to you. Personality tests (such as the MBTI or the Big Five Personality Traits) are often used as team-building exercises at work or in recruitment to establish if a candidate will fit into a team, and to help existing team members identify their natural competencies.

Understanding different personality types can also assist you in tailoring your communication style to each person. Factors like extraversion or introversion may affect how somebody relates to you and how open or closed they are to a particular communication technique. Awareness of personality differences is also invaluable in conflict resolution: every person has different triggers and values, and experienced managers and negotiators know to work with this.

Questions in Personality

Dr Shigehiro Oishi, Marshall Field IV Professor of Psychology at the University of Chicago, studies personality across cultures and asks, "Who is more happy, extraverts or introverts?"

Extraverts are happier, he says, and this finding has been replicated often in the United States. However, research has found that in Germany and Japan, extraverts are not much happier than introverts. One explanation for the discrepancy is that in the United States extraverts have a social advantage because of the individualistic nature of that society, whereas in Germany and Japan, people's social networks remain pretty much the same from childhood to adulthood because they don't move around as much, and there's less reward to be had from talking with strangers.

Most personality research has historically been conducted in Western Europe and the United States, across certain demographics, carrying certain biases, so cross-cultural studies are vital to arriving at a wider understanding of personality in action.

PERSONALITY THEORIES

Fashions come and go, and so do different schools of thought around how to define, describe and understand human personality. Many theories were developed by white, middle- or upper-class men in the nineteenth and twentieth centuries, and as you read through them, you may find yourself wondering whether such narrow frames of reference could possibly serve humans as a whole. Women and people of colour are noticeably absent from many psychology textbooks; much early work on the documentation of different cultures and practices comes from a white gaze and colonial perspective. In seeking to include underacknowledged contributions to psychology, it is encouraging to see a greater breadth, depth and increasing diversity in the field today.

Like many concepts in psychology, theories of personality have evolved over time, often building on and incorporating pieces of prior work. Sometimes, like in other branches of sciences, there is a paradigm shift, but often changes in thinking are more gradual, and several similar theories intersect and overlap. Here are a few of them...

Psychoanalytic Theories

Psychoanalytic theories, characterized by the thinking of Sigmund Freud, are part of a wider group known as psychodynamic theories which include those of Freud's followers and thinkers who built on his initial ideas, such as Alfred Adler, Carl Jung and Karen Horney. While psychoanalytic theories focus on the unconscious mind and include the role of sexuality, psychodynamic theories emphasize the social environment to a greater extent.

Freud's psychoanalytic theory introduced the idea that the unconscious mind is involved in shaping personality and behaviour. His structural model of the psyche and theses on defence mechanisms and developmental stages form the foundation of his approach. He saw the personality as comprising three parts: the id, the ego and the superego, and he emphasized the importance of early childhood experiences, particularly in the formation of unconscious desires and conflict. Such concepts were both groundbreaking and controversial at the time and continue to drive debate and divide schools of thought.

Sigmund Freud used an iceberg to represent his theory of the tripartite personality, which consists of the id, the ego and the superego. Most of the iceberg lies under the water, representing our unconscious mind. You can read more about Freud's theories in *The Little Book of Psychology* (Summersdale, 2019).

SIGMUND FREUD

1856–1939

BIOGRAPHY

Born in Freiberg in the Austrian Empire (now Příbor, Czech Republic), Sigmund Freud moved with his Jewish family to Vienna in 1860, where he stayed until the Nazi annexation of Austria in 1938. Entering the University of Vienna to study medicine, he trained in psychiatry and internal medicine and in 1885 was appointed lecturer in neuropathology. His scientific background and dedication to experimentation were crucial to his approach, and Freud's trip to Paris later that year, during which time he was introduced to Jean-Martin Charcot's work with "hysterical" patients using hypnosis, led him to believe that a new psychological method of analysis was possible. In the early 1900s Freud's psychoanalytic method drew a circle of supporters, who would meet in his waiting room every Wednesday – among them Adler, Jung and Ferenczi – a group which would become the Vienna Psychoanalytic Society.

Freud published many seminal books and papers, including 1900's *The Interpretation of Dreams* and 1923's *The Ego and the Id (Structures of Personality)*. After being forced to flee Austria, Freud settled in England and died not long after the outbreak of the Second World War.

SIGNIFICANCE IN PSYCHOLOGY

Freud is known as the father of psychoanalysis and it's no understatement to say that his work on the unconscious mind and personality laid the foundation for modern psychological practice. Freud built on early work done with Josef Breuer to popularize talking therapy as a clinical practice, and while many of Freud's followers and modern practitioners would disagree with his theories about psychosexual stages and human behaviour as a manifestation of repressed sexual desire, there's no doubt his scientific mindset and willingness to upset traditional beliefs about the nature of the psyche are just as important today as they were 100 years ago.

The Neo-Freudians

The popularity of Freud's theories and his leadership of the new Vienna Psychoanalytic Society meant that he had many followers, some of whom would adapt his theories and become important figures in personality psychology themselves. Most of them were more optimistic than Freud about the prospects for people to shape their personality in adulthood, leaning less on theories about sexuality as a motivating force.

Anna Freud (1895–1982) was Sigmund Freud's youngest daughter and is considered one of the founders of child psychology. Her work emphasized the development of the ego and took a collaborative approach. When the family fled Austria, she settled in London, where she set up the Hampstead War Nurseries for children with Dorothy Burlingham (1891–1979), and offered staff psychoanalytic training. Their work with children and observational studies led them to establish the clinic as a centre for training, research and development (today the Anna Freud National Centre for Children and Families).

Alfred Adler (1870–1937) interpreted Freudian theory in order to claim that an inferiority complex stemming from childhood neglect could be a cause of most psychological disorders, as sufferers attempt to compensate by asserting their superiority over others.

Karen Horney (1855–1952) was a German physician whose personality theory took a more balanced view of the sexes. The first woman trained as a Freudian psychoanalyst, she argued that Freudian theories were inherently biased against women and loaded by women's dependency on men. For example, Freud believed that boys pass through a phallic stage in which they desire their mother (Oedipus complex), while girls experience jealousy at not having a penis. Horney's personality theory is based on people's desire for security and ability to develop supportive relationships. Her term "basic anxiety" influenced fellow neo-Freudian Erik Erikson's (1902–1994) idea of "basic mistrust", which became his first stage of psychosocial development.

Carl Jung (1875–1961) was another student of Freud who went on to develop his own personality theories based not on sex, but on archetypes rooted in the collective unconscious. We cover Jung's theories on page 32.

Trait Theories

Personality is difficult to measure, and psychologists have always argued about which "units" to use. Trait theories focus on identifying and categorizing enduring personality traits that characterize individuals' behaviour across various situations. American psychologist Gordon Allport was the first person to formally introduce the idea of traits as a way to describe the stable dimensions of personality, and his *Personality: A Psychological Interpretation* (1937) became an influential textbook, building on existing European research and theory and naming over 4,000 traits. Traits are continuous factors such as field dependence (when someone relies more on environmental cues than on bodily sensation cues), sensation-seeking and achievement motivation, and trait theory says that measuring these traits can predict future behaviour.

In 1968, Walter Mischel (1930–2018) argued that, when it came to determining someone's personality, any given situation was more influential than a trait. There followed a boom in the popularity of social psychology, which prioritized the role of situations and surroundings in shaping personality. Since then, the field has grown and diversified, with trait models and theories spanning and drawing from interrelated sub-fields including cognitive behaviourism and biological theories of personality. Traits are also defined relative to a person's thoughts or beliefs about their own capabilities (self-efficacy) – a concept developed further by cognitive behaviourists.

> *We don't see things as they are. We see things as we are.*
>
> **ANAÏS NIN**

The Big Five

Trait theorist Raymond Cattell (1905-1998) reduced the number of main personality traits from Allport's initial list of over 4,000 down to 171, mostly by eliminating uncommon traits and combining common ones. Cattell then rated a large sample of individuals for these 171 different traits. Then, using a statistical technique known as factor analysis, he identified closely related terms, reducing his list to 16 key personality traits. Other psychologists reduced these 16 traits to just five. Among them were Donald Fiske, Lewis Goldberg and Robert McCrae and Paul Costa, who provided the model used today: Openness, Conscientiousness, Extraversion, Agreeableness and Neuroticism – OCEAN, or CANOE, for short.

The model became known as the "Big Five" and has received much attention. It has been researched across many populations and cultures and continues to be the most widely accepted theory of personality today. Currently, behavioural psychologists use these traits to profile social media users and predict their behaviour, with sometimes impressive accuracy, although there is evidence that the model doesn't stand up as well outside the culture it was based on. We will explore the "Big Five" in more detail on page 85.

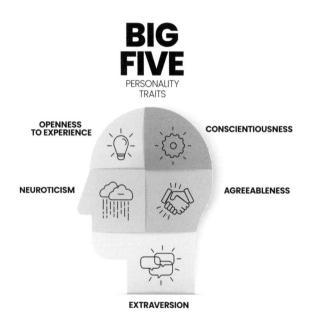

GORDON ALLPORT

1897–1967

BIOGRAPHY

Gordon Allport was an American psychologist and teacher who significantly shaped both personality psychology and social psychology. Born in Montezuma, Indiana, he was influenced by his older brother Floyd, noted psychologist. After graduating from Harvard, Allport taught in Turkey and studied in Germany and the UK. A meeting with Sigmund Freud in Vienna prompted him to challenge the prevailing psychoanalytic approach of digging into the unconscious mind, and Allport began to develop his own theories about how behaviour is affected by the more current, conscious motivations of a person. Returning to Harvard to pursue his doctoral studies, Allport was elected president of the American Psychological Association in 1939. Throughout his long teaching career in America, he was known for his warmth, wit, ethical approach and nondogmatic humanism.

SIGNIFICANCE IN PSYCHOLOGY

Allport's trait theory revolutionized the understanding of personality by proposing that individuals possess unique combinations of traits that shape their behaviour and responses.

His 1937 book *Personality* remained an important textbook in psychology and he edited and retitled it in 1961 as *Pattern and Growth in Personality.* Allport identified over 3,000 trait-like words in personality and classified them into three levels:

- A cardinal trait dominates and shapes a person's behaviour (rare, as most of us lack a single overriding trait).

- A central trait is a general characteristic found in all of us and a building block of personality (for example, honesty).

- A secondary trait is a characteristic seen only in some circumstances, but nevertheless important for illustrating human complexity.

Type Theories

While trait theory identifies characteristics which are shared to some degree across most people, type theory seeks to identify and categorize people by personality type into distinct groups. While traits may have intrinsic negative or positive connotations, types are neutral in their definition and each type identifies normal, healthy behaviours relating to the way each person takes in information, makes choices and relates to the world.

Carl Jung is largely classified as a psychodynamic theorist, but his work on types is worth highlighting. Apart from Freud, Jung's influences stretched back to antiquity and encompassed the more recent philosopher Friedrich Nietzsche and psychologist William James. Jung thought that personality theories to some extent could be expressed through the personality type of the theorist. For example, he saw Freud as an extravert and described his theory as "centrifugal", while Allport's "centripetal" theory was due to his introversion. Jung wanted to create his own psychology which would be fair to both types.

Jung suggested that people experience the world using four principal psychological functions – sensing, intuition, feeling and thinking – each of which can be expressed in an introverted or extraverted form, and that one of these four functions is dominant for a person most of the time. Jung classified himself as an introverted thinker with intuition as his next strongest function, and identified eight main personality types:

1. **Extraverted Thinking**
   Principled, idealistic, objective, rational.
2. **Introverted Thinking**
   Influenced by ideas, independent, often fearful of intimacy.
3. **Extraverted Feeling**
   Adaptive, relating well to the external.
4. **Introverted Feeling**
   Sympathetic, pleases others, may be dependent, reserved.
5. **Extraverted Sensation**
   Realistic, concrete, pleasant and friendly.
6. **Introverted Sensation**
   Calm and passive, restrained, controlled and controlling.
7. **Extraverted Intuition**
   Enterprising, outgoing, can be irresponsible.
8. **Introverted Intuition**
   Mystical, dreamer and artist. Can be obsessive.

CARL JUNG

1875–1961

BIOGRAPHY

Carl Jung was born in Kesswil, Switzerland. Instead of following his father into the clergy, Jung studied in Basel and then Zurich, where he worked with pioneering psychologist Eugen Bleuler at Burgholzli Asylum. Establishing a reputation as a psychologist with an interest in the subconscious, Jung followed Freud's ideas and eventually worked closely with him from 1907–1912, after which Jung published *Psychology of the Unconscious*, which challenged a number of Freud's theories directly. This break with Freud led to Jung resigning from the International Psychoanalytic Association in 1914. Travelling widely in later years, Jung studied other cultures and published over 200 works on his theories including 1957's *The Undiscovered Self*. Jung held professorships at the Federal Polytechnic in Zurich and the University of Basel, and in 1938 was elected honorary fellow of the UK's Royal Society of Medicine. After a long marriage to

Emma Rauschenbach, with whom he had five children, Jung died in Zurich in 1961.

SIGNIFICANCE IN PSYCHOLOGY

Jung coined the term "analytical psychology" and, as one of the key neo-Freudians, established distinct ideas on archetypes, the collective unconscious and the individuation process, by which we grow into our "true self". Jung introduced the concept of psychological types and the distinction between introversion and extraversion. His typology expanded the understanding of personality by proposing that individuals exhibit distinct preferences in perceiving and judging information, impacting their behaviour and interpersonal dynamics.

KATHARINE BRIGGS AND ISABEL BRIGGS MYERS

KATHARINE BRIGGS: 1875–1968
ISABEL BRIGGS MYERS: 1897–1980

BIOGRAPHY

Katharine Briggs (neé Cook) was a magazine and essay writer, housewife and correspondent of Jung's. Born in Michigan, USA, Briggs studied Jung's theories on personality types and started work on her own system of classifying his types into a more extensive personality system. When her daughter Isabel was born, Katharine homeschooled her and kept detailed observations on her development. After graduating with a degree in political science, Isabel began working with her mother to create their personality questionnaire. Referencing Jung's eight types, the questionnaire posited 16 personality types which could be used to profile and select workers for suitable roles.

SIGNIFICANCE IN PSYCHOLOGY

The women patented the Myers-Briggs Type Indicator (MBTI) and Isabel worked with the Educational Testing Service in Princeton to publish it. In 1975, Isabel co-founded CAPT (Center for Applications of Psychological Type) in Gainesville, Florida, with Mary McCaulley, PhD, a faculty in clinical psychology at University of Florida.

The MBTI became a bestseller, available in 29 languages, and has been used in 115 countries by a wide range of businesses, academic institutions, job placement organizations and even by services that pair roommates at college. Like Jung's types, the 16 types of the MBTI do not carry any positive or negative association, but are judgement-free.

Humanistic Theories

As the field of personality psychology developed in the early twentieth century, much of the thinking came out of the psychoanalytic approach of Freud, Jung and colleagues, whose primary sources were the patients they saw in their clinics. However, humanists including Abraham Maslow and Carl Rogers thought it was also important to study the personalities of people who weren't in therapy or seeking help. The new focus was on understanding and promoting individual strengths like happiness and creativity, and examining the environment that makes these strengths more likely to progress positively.

The humanistic theory of personality states that people are basically good and want to become their best selves. Each of us has an inborn goodness and is motivated towards self-improvement, but each of us can also be held back from self-actualization (completely realizing one's potential) by our environment. For example, the psychologists Kenneth and Mamie Clark conducted trailblazing research in 1950s America on Black children's self-esteem, which demonstrated that that racism and segregation caused personality damage. The Clarks'

findings led directly to policy change and the beginnings of desegregation in learning.

Humanistic theory contends that the way a person chooses to behave is directly influenced by their self-concept, environment and past experiences.

Humanistic psychology is made up of five core principles:

1. Human beings supersede the sum of their parts.

2. Each human is unique.

3. Human beings are aware and conscious beings with the capacity for self-awareness.

4. Human beings have free will, can make their own choices and are responsible for their own choices.

5. Human beings intentionally work to achieve future goals. They also seek meaning, creativity and value in life.

ABRAHAM MASLOW

1908–1970

BIOGRAPHY

Abraham Maslow was born in New York to Russian–Jewish immigrants. He studied psychology at the University of Wisconsin and then gestalt psychology (a school of psychology based on the idea that what we experience is greater than the sum of its parts) in New York, eventually becoming head of the psychology department at Brandeis University.

SIGNIFICANCE IN PSYCHOLOGY

Maslow co-founded the *Journal of Humanistic Psychology* in 1961 and the *Journal of Transpersonal Psychology* in 1969. His most famous work, Maslow's Hierarchy of Needs, places each human need one on top of another in pyramid form, starting at the bottom and moving up, with the first levels of need monopolizing consciousness until they are met, after which the mind can move up to the next level, eventually achieving self-actualization.

Maslow's Hierarchy of Needs

SELF-ACTUALIZATION

ESTEEM

SOCIAL BELONGING

SAFETY NEEDS

PHYSIOLOGICAL NEEDS

Social Cognitive Theories

Social cognitive theories of personality try to explain how people learn and behave, and develop their personalities, exploring the interplay between individuals' cognitive processes, social environments and behaviour. The theory suggests that the relationship between individuals and their environment is bidirectional, so behaviour is influenced by a continuous interaction between personal factors, environmental stimuli and cognitive processes.

The theory of behaviourism (see page 44) emerged in the early twentieth century. Ivan Pavlov (1849–1936) and B. F. Skinner believed that observable behaviours could be studied scientifically, without needing to delve into thoughts or feelings. They focused on how behaviours are shaped by rewards, punishments and environmental influences, rather than thoughts or innate knowledge.

However, in the 1960s, psychologists began to speculate that there was more to behaviour than just external factors. Albert Bandura, one of the pioneers of social cognitive theory, introduced the concept of observational learning. He showed that people learn by watching others, not just through their own experiences. This idea challenged the strict behaviourist view and opened the door to a new understanding of human behaviour.

Bandura's work laid the foundation for social cognitive theory, which suggests that behaviour is influenced by a combination of personal factors, environmental factors and cognitive processes. In other words, our thoughts, beliefs and perceptions play a crucial role in shaping how we behave.

As the field continued to evolve, researchers like Jacquelynne Eccles and Allan Wigfield further expanded social cognitive theory by exploring concepts like expectancy and value. They showed that learners' choices and actions are guided by their expectations of outcomes and the importance they place on those outcomes, within the framework of the students' goals, interests, sense of self-efficacy and feeling of self-determination.

Over time, social cognitive theories have become increasingly sophisticated, incorporating insights from neuroscience, cognitive psychology and other disciplines. Today, they are widely used to understand everything from personality development to social influence to health behaviour.

Behaviourism

The emergence of the theory of behaviourism sparked intense debate, especially in education, where its application was the most easily tested. This school of thought strongly rejected the idea that we have innate knowledge of our unconscious drivers of behaviour, in favour of the conviction that everything we know is a result of our learning and conditioning, and the particular environment we are placed in.

Classical conditioning involves the subject beginning to form an association between a previously neutral environmental stimulus (like a light being switched on) and a naturally occurring stimulus (like a dog salivating when food touches its tongue). It was first described by Russian psychologist Ivan Pavlov who, while studying the digestive system of dogs, discovered he could make them drool in response to a stimulus, hence the popular term "Pavlov's dog".

In 1913, John B. Watson published what was considered the "behaviourist manifesto", a book called *Psychology as the Behaviorist Views It*. He is famous for an experiment in classical conditioning on a small boy known as "Little Albert".

In Watson's study on 11-month-old "Little Albert", he and his assistant Rosalie Rayner conditioned the toddler to become afraid of a white rat by creating loud noises behind Albert's back every time the rat was produced. Initially, Albert didn't fear the rat, but soon began to cry (without any accompanying loud noise) not just at the sight of the rat, but at any small white creature which resembled it. The boy was never deconditioned, unfortunately – something that would be unethical in any experiment today.

B. F. Skinner, who expanded on the work of Edward Thorndike, was the first to study the effect of reinforcement on behaviour. His theory of operant conditioning is one of the most important aspects of his approach to behaviourism. Skinner tested mice to see how they responded to different sorts of conditioning, and discovered that the behaviour of the mice would change in response to either positive reinforcement (rewarding good behaviour) or negative reinforcement (removing something unpleasant when good behaviour occurs). The environment he set up for the mice became known as the Skinner Box. Skinner thought he could use this to help students learn more skills.

One other precept of behaviourism is that there is no difference across species – the principles of learning are the same.

The fact that animals do in fact learn in different ways was part of the argument against behaviourism. The theory was further debunked in a scathing book review by Noam Chomsky, which argued that it made no allowance for people's interior world, neglecting their cognitive processes, and that excessive reliance on external rewards would lead to a diminished intrinsic motivation. After the pinnacle of its popularity between the two world wars, behaviourism gradually became eclipsed by cognitive and humanistic movements in psychology. Behaviourism underpins interventions such as Applied Behaviour Analysis (ABA) and more recently Naturalistic Development Behavioural Interventions (NDBIs), which are used as tools by professionals working with autistic children.

Education is what survives when what has been learned has been forgotten.

B. F. SKINNER, *NEW METHODS AND NEW AIMS IN TEACHING*

B. F. SKINNER

1904–1990

BIOGRAPHY

Burrhus Frederic Skinner was born in Pennsylvania, USA, and earned his doctorate in psychology at Harvard. He published *The Behavior of Organisms* in 1938, based on his experiments in operant conditioning. After serving as chair of psychology at Indiana University, he spent the rest of his career as a Harvard professor. He published a novel that extolled his views on behaviour called *Walden Two* (1948), and responded to Chomsky's criticism of his ideas in the 1974 work *About Behaviorism*.

SIGNIFICANCE IN PSYCHOLOGY

Skinner's research into behaviourism remains relevant. His work with the Skinner Box, a piece of laboratory equipment used to observe animal behaviour, and subsequent identification of the importance of reinforcement, has proven to be critical. Positive reinforcement is still used to shape behaviour in education today.

Social Learning Theories

Psychologist Albert Bandura developed the social learning theory in response to the limitations of behavioural theories of learning. He recognized that people learn not just by direct reinforcement and the variables within their own environment, but also by observing how others behave, how and when they receive punishment, and by imitation.

This learning occurs within a social environment, resulting from a shared interaction between person, environment and behaviour. The theory is useful in explaining how children learn by imitating family members, friends and other influencers.

Whether applied to education, social work or criminology, social learning theory is effective and can be used with other ideas and practices to bring about change.

Some foundational ideas connected with social learning theory are:

1. People learn through observation.
2. Reinforcement and punishment have an indirect effect on behaviour and learning.

3. Cognitive factors contribute to whether a behaviour is acquired.

4. Learning involves modelling, yet does not require behavioural change.

Importantly, this research shows that humans can learn without directly experiencing the consequences of their own actions; that learning is observational and depends on how a behaviour is modelled, even if indirectly.

ALBERT BANDURA

1925–2021

BIOGRAPHY

Albert Bandura, a Canadian-American psychologist, was the youngest son of Eastern European parents who had settled in Canada. He graduated in psychology in 1949 from the University of British Columbia, before undertaking doctoral studies at the University of Iowa. He quickly became a professor at Stanford University, where he remained until 2010. He received numerous awards for contributions to the field of psychology, and was actively publishing books and journals into his nineties.

SIGNIFICANCE IN PSYCHOLOGY

Bandura's social learning theory emphasized the role of observational learning and cognitive processes in behaviour. His research on modelling and self-efficacy expanded the understanding of human behaviour, and he was called to testify on the effects of televised violence after the assassination of Senator Robert F. Kennedy in 1968.

The Bobo Doll Experiment

Bandura's most famous study is the Bobo doll experiment, conducted in 1961 at the Stanford University nursery school, which examined how children responded to researchers modelling abusive behaviour. Children aged from three to six watched as researchers physically and verbally abused a clown-faced inflatable toy, and later mimicked the abusive behaviour, imitating the exact behaviour they had witnessed in the adult. Those children who were in a non-aggressive group, in which they witnessed the researchers ignoring the Bobo doll and playing calmly with other toys, did not exhibit the aggression shown by the first group.

Later the experiment was repeated, only this time the children were shown the abuse on videotape. They again mimicked the modelled behaviour, and were more likely to be abusive or violent if they had witnessed the adult modelling the behaviour being rewarded or praised for it.

In a follow-up study in 1965, Bandura also found that children were far less likely to imitate aggression and violence if they saw an adult model being punished or reprimanded for their hostile behaviour.

Expectancy–Value Theory

Expectancy-value theory was developed by Jacquelynne Eccles, Allan Wigfield and their colleagues, and highlights which factors people prioritize when they decide whether to undertake a task or learning activity. These are:

1. Expectations for success: for example, if a child believes they're good at multiplication, they're more likely to enjoy doing sums.

2. Subjective task value: this is about how much they care about the activity or task. There are four parts to this:

    - Attainment value: how important it is for them to do well in the task.

    - Intrinsic value: how much they personally enjoy the task.

    - Utility value: how useful they think the task is for their future goals.

    - Cost: what they might have to give up to do the task, like time spent on other things.

Eccles and her colleagues showed that when children decide whether to do something, they think about how well they think they'll do at it and how much they care about it. Children tend to value the domains in which they feel competent, and also take into account the opinions of those around them.

They also showed that expectations for success (i.e. competence-related beliefs) are more strongly linked to performance. For example, a girl who believes she will do well in maths tends to get higher grades than a girl who does not expect to do well.

Task values are more strongly tied to achievement-related choices. For example, a girl who values maths is more likely to take advanced maths courses than a girl who does not value it. So expectancy–value theory highlights the dual importance of expectations for success and values in explaining children's motivation.

JACQUELYNNE ECCLES

BORN 1944

BIOGRAPHY

Jacquelynne Eccles is the Distinguished Professor of Education at the University of California, Irvine. She earned her PhD in developmental psychology from the University of California in 1974. She was awarded the APA Distinguished Scientific Award for the Applications of Psychology from the American Psychological Association in 2017.

SIGNIFICANCE IN PSYCHOLOGY

Eccles is known for her work on expectancy-value theory, focusing on motivation and achievement in educational settings. Her research highlighted the importance of individuals' beliefs and values, as well as gender roles, in shaping their goals and behaviour. This research provided insights into motivation and achievement in various domains, influencing educational practices and research on goal pursuit.

While many areas of the brain work in conjunction most of the time, different lobes are largely responsible for different functions. In addition to the frontal and parietal lobes, each hemisphere has a temporal lobe – important for hearing, recognizing language and forming memories – and an occipital lobe, the brain's major visual processing centre.

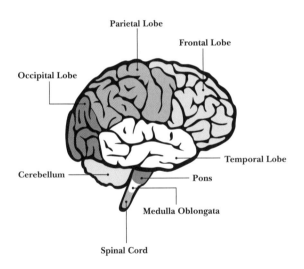

Biological Theories

You've probably heard the expression "nature vs nurture", but what do we mean when we say that? Imagine a set of identical twins who are separated at birth and grow up in different cultures or home environments. Genetically, their brains may be identical, but the environment they are raised in – the "nurture" aspect – is not the same at all. How do you think their personalities would develop?

The biological basis of personality emphasizes the internal physiological and genetic factors that influence personality (the "nature" aspect). Relevant here are links between DNA, processes in the brain and personality. In the example above, one twin may be a "loner" and have trouble relating to those around them. The other may be part of a strong community and feel socially close to others, whereas both twins may have similarly vivid imaginations. Identical twin research has shown that social closeness is a trait minimally influenced by genetics, while imagination is strongly influenced.

In the past it was almost impossible to see what goes on inside a living person's brain, but today we have powerful techniques such as fMRI (functional MRI), which can show us how different areas in our brain light up when activated by various stimuli. Researchers used to have to rely on learning from freak accidents, such as how a person's personality changed after a brain injury – the most famous example being that of Phineas Gage, who survived an iron pole piercing his skull and damaging his frontal lobe. It was perhaps the first case to demonstrate which specific parts of the brain, when affected, can induce specific personality changes.

Now, neuropsychologists can study in detail how the structure of the brain is related to psychological processes and behaviours. For instance, in human beings, the frontal lobe is responsible for foresight and anticipation, while the parietal lobe is a major sensory processing hub for your brain, making sense of language and combining information from multiple senses into a usable form.

Three-Factor Model of Personality

One of the best known biological theorists was Hans Eysenck, who believed that personality traits are linked to neural mechanisms and brain structures, which in turn affect how we behave and what motivates us. Eysenck's three-factor model of personality breaks down personality into the following dimensions:

Extraversion (E): This dimension describes how outgoing and sociable a person is. Those high in extraversion tend to be energetic, talkative and seek out social interactions due to low cortical arousal, while those low in extraversion are more reserved and prefer solitude, with high cortical arousal leading them to avoid stimulation.

Neuroticism (N): Neuroticism refers to the degree of emotional instability and negative emotionality in a person. Individuals high in neuroticism experience higher levels of anxiety, moodiness and emotional volatility, whereas those low in neuroticism tend to be more emotionally stable and resilient.

Eysenck used a statistical technique known as factor analysis to identify these first two factors of personality, and later added a third factor:

Psychoticism (P): This dimension represents traits such as aggressiveness, impulsivity and a tendency towards antisocial behaviour. High levels of psychoticism indicate a greater propensity for unconventional or even hostile behaviour, whereas low levels suggest greater social conformity and empathy.

While Eysenck's theory is backed up by research and shown to be stable across time and cultures, some criticized it for being too simplistic and not taking into account other aspects of personality such as openness to experience and conscientiousness (both factors which are included in the OCEAN, or Big Five, model).

Other notable biological theories include Jeffrey Alan Gray's reinforcement sensitivity theory, and C. Robert Cloninger's psychobiological theory of personality, a seven-factor model that includes four dimensions of temperament and three dimensions of character. Like Eysenck's theory, these seven factors are linked to biological systems and thought to be inherited.

Emerging neuroscience evidence shows that pleasure, pain and other emotions have different neural pathways, helping theorists understand why people differ in their reaction to the same events.

HANS EYSENCK

1916–1997

BIOGRAPHY

Born in Germany and raised by his grandparents, Eysenck moved to England aged 18, where he earned a PhD in psychology from University College London in 1940. From 1955–1983 he was a professor at the Institute of Psychiatry, continuing to work until his death. During his (sometimes controversial) career he published more than 70 books and 1,600 scientific articles.

SIGNIFICANCE IN PSYCHOLOGY

Eysenck's three-factor theory of personality was based on his work on temperament, which he believed was controlled by genetic influences, playing an important role in establishing empirical approaches to clinical training. He was deeply critical of Freudian psychoanalysis and dismissed it as unscientific. In a 1952 paper, he wrote that two-thirds of therapy patients significantly improved or recovered within two years, regardless of whether they received psychotherapy or not.

Eysenck was also the subject of much controversy for his views on race and intelligence in particular. He wrote that racial differences in intelligence could be partially attributed to genetic factors, and his 1971 book *The IQ Argument: Race, Intelligence, and Education* prompted a great deal of criticism. Later in autobiographical work, he took a moderate approach. By the time of his death in 1997, Eysenck was the most frequently cited psychologist in scientific journals.

Evolutionary Theory

Charles Darwin is famous for his theory of natural selection. In 1873, he argued that human emotional expressions likely evolved in the same way as physical features do. In biological heredity, features like brown eyes, webbed feet, eyesight and hearing evolved in order to help us to survive and thrive. Evolutionary psychologists look at how not just biological characteristics, but also cognitive traits are passed down through generations as a survival mechanism.

Evolutionary psychology posits why things like empathy, fear of the dark, generosity, partner preference, anxiousness and honesty might have been preserved via natural selection traced back to factors essential to survival in a small community.

Two of the most influential evolutionary psychologists are Leda Cosmides and John Tooby. In *The Handbook of Evolutionary Psychology* (2015) they write:

> "The brain's function is specifically computational: to regulate behavior, development, and the body in ways that would have produced responses likely to have promoted genetic propagation under ancestral conditions."

CHARLES DARWIN

1809–1882

BIOGRAPHY

Darwin was born in Shrewsbury, England. He went to study medicine at Edinburgh University, before eventually transferring to Christ's College, Cambridge.

Darwin then joined HMS *Beagle's* circumnavigation of the world, collecting zoological specimens and later publishing the groundbreaking *On the Origin of Species* in 1859.

SIGNIFICANCE IN PSYCHOLOGY

Darwin's concept of natural selection underscored the importance of different individual characteristics in survival, spurring interest in the study of variations in personality, intelligence and behaviour.

Evolutionary theory has had a profound influence on the science of psychology. Both fields hold that genes not only code for specific traits but also influence patterns of cognition and behaviour.

Attachment Theory

Opposing the dominance of behavioural theory in psychology and parenting advice in the mid-twentieth century, another school of thought emerged around how infants develop attachment to their primary caregiver. Like the behaviours discussed in evolutionary theory, attachment theorists John Bowlby and Mary Ainsworth proposed that human babies had evolved to seek proximity and security when stressed, whether due to internal or external factors.

During early childhood, this need for a secure attachment is at its highest. Ainsworth's doctoral advisor William Blatz had already developed ideas about security in infancy, and she and the psychiatrist John Bowlby built on Blatz's theory to outline the four styles of attachment in infants (see page 65). These styles would go on to influence how people relate to other people and situations as adults, how they operate in intimate relationships and how they parent their children. Many contemporary psychologists and researchers use attachment theory in their practice today.

MARY AINSWORTH

1913–1999

BIOGRAPHY

Born in Ohio, USA, but raised in Ontario, Canada, Mary Ainsworth earned her doctorate in psychology in 1939. After teaching at the University of Toronto, she moved to London in 1950 and met John Bowlby. Together they fashioned new ideas about attachment theory. In 1967, Ainsworth published *Infancy in Uganda: Infant Care and the Growth of Love*.

SIGNIFICANCE TO PSYCHOLOGY

This research ultimately led to her development of the four attachment styles. These are secure attachment, disorganized attachment in infants who are inconsistent in their behaviour, and two types of insecure attachment: anxious-avoidant and anxious-resident.

Ainsworth's insights led not just to a new area of research in psychology, but to a change in popular parenting styles and official advice, too.

PERSONALITY TESTS

Numerous personality tests are conducted today, as part of assessment or therapy, in schools or workplaces, or out of curiosity. More insidiously, it's likely that an algorithm has been used to classify you or assign you a score for some trait without your explicit knowledge: think about credit scoring, social media recommendations or advertising.

When an academic study using Facebook profiles and personality testing was mobilized by a campaign in the 2016 US election, the press claimed, "Facebook knows you better than your friends do."

In this chapter, we'll look at the two main groups of personality tests – projective and objective – and find out what they aim to do and why they're useful.

This book does not provide the tests themselves. Many of them are available online in a self-report version, while others are only used by qualified health professionals.

Projective Tests

Projective tests of personality have their origins in psychoanalytic theory, and assume that personality is primarily unconscious and therefore not directly accessible. Instead of closed questions, projective tests are ambiguous in the stimuli they offer, and they aim to prompt the person doing the test to access some hidden or unconscious feeling, wish or conflict. By interpreting responses to these cues, psychoanalysts try to identify recurring themes, symbols or patterns that may provide insights into the individual's personality traits, emotional states, conflicts or underlying psychological issues. Common examples include the Rorschach inkblot and Thematic Apperception Test (TAT).

Although their use has declined, projective tests are still used in clinical psychology, counselling and psychotherapy, as well as forensic settings. They are often used with other assessment methods to provide a comprehensive understanding of psychological functioning.

Criticism of these tests – namely that they lack standardized administration and scoring procedures, making them subjective and prone to interpretation bias – has done little to stem their appeal in popular culture, and you are much more likely to see an inkblot test used as a prop in a film than any of the objective tests.

An inkblot inspired by the Rorschach test

The Rorschach Inkblot Test

Invented by the Swiss psychiatrist Hermann Rorschach, the test measures our general approach to perception. While working in a mental institution in Switzerland, he made some inkblot paintings, asking ill patients "what might this be?" He wanted to know how people view and organize the world around them.

Rorschach developed a system to code the responses and quantify the test-takers. Qualities like the following could be evaluated:

- The person's emotional world
- The person's cognitive world
- The person's ability to deal with situational stress
- The person's perception of others and relationships
- The person's self-perception

Rorschach published his coding system in 1921, but died suddenly in 1922 aged 37. After that, the test began to be used in ways he hadn't intended, and there was little quality control of the evaluation of the results. A large-scale 2013 review of existing research showed that when used properly the inkblot test can give valid results.

The Thematic Apperception Test (TAT)

The TAT is a tool designed to reveal a person's underlying motives, concerns and desires. In the test, the subject is shown a series of picture cards depicting various ambiguous characters, scenes and situations. They are then prompted to make up stories based on these images, offering insights into their subconscious thoughts and feelings. These stories should describe:

- What has led up to the event depicted
- What is happening in the picture
- How the characters are thinking and feeling
- How the story ends

The narratives the subject develops provide clinicians with valuable information about their personality, emotions, conflicts and interpersonal relationships, and gives more context and detail than the inkblot test alone. Originally, the TAT was designed with 31 cards, and was designed for a subset of these to be used with each subject. Although it's primarily aimed at those over 14, there is a version for younger people.

More About the TAT

The TAT was developed in the 1930s by Henry Murray and Christiana Morgan, who wanted to assess personality characteristics that could not be captured by more traditional measures. The TAT analyzes an individual's inner world, exploring themes such as power, achievement, intimacy and interpersonal dynamics.

Despite its widespread use and popularity among clinicians, the TAT has also faced criticism regarding its reliability and validity. Some argue that the subjective nature of interpreting responses introduces bias and limits the test's objectivity. Additionally, there are concerns about the cultural and gender biases inherent in the test's stimuli and scoring criteria.

But proponents of the TAT emphasize its value in psychotherapy and counselling, where it allows the person viewing the image to control how the story they've constructed turns out. By uncovering unconscious thoughts and motivations, the test can help therapists to formulate treatment plans and encourage self-awareness in patients. The test is often used with a sub-selection of images catering to patient-specific situations.

The Draw-a-Person Test

This test builds on the "Draw-a-Man" test created by Florence Goodenough in 1926. The test subject is asked to draw a person. The subject might be prompted with further instructions like drawing a man, woman or child. The test's simplicity means it is often used with children. If they draw more than one person, different sheets of paper are used. Open-ended questions can then be asked, such as:

- Who is in the drawing?
- What are they doing?
- What are they thinking and feeling?

The test is then scored by noting the answers to the questions and examining elements like the size of body parts, the level of detail given to the figure, as well as the form and scale of the drawing.

Like other projective tests, the Draw-a-Person test has been criticized for its lack of validity. It is mostly used to evaluate cognitive development in children and also gives insights into personality, self-image and family relationships. The test can be used to evaluate stroke patients.

The House-Tree-Person Test

In another simple test, a person is asked to draw a house, a tree and a person. Once they have finished the drawing, they are asked a series of questions about what they have drawn.

The test was originally designed by John Buck in 1948, building on the Goodenough test, and included a series of 60 questions to ask the respondent. Test administrators may also come up with their own questions or follow-up queries to further explore the subject's responses. For example, the administrator might ask:

ABOUT THE HOUSE:

- Who lives here?
- Who visits the person who lives here?

ABOUT THE TREE:

- What kind of tree is it?
- Who waters the tree?

AND ABOUT THE PERSON:

- How old are they?
- Do they feel happy?

Each part of the drawing – the house, the tree and the person – has its own set of associated scoring criteria. For example, if a person draws a tiny house, that could be interpreted as unhappiness with life at home. A tree lacking branches might reflect solitariness, and the hands of the person could give clues to how aggressive the person taking the test is.

A house-tree-person test can be scored either in an objective quantitative or subjective qualitative manner. In a formal therapy setting, Buck's 350-page manual and interpretative guide is used to administer and score the test, and this quantitative scoring gives a general assessment of intelligence. The test can be an effective tool in evaluating brain damage in patients with schizophrenia. When scored qualitatively, it shows little evidence of validity.

Objective Tests

Objective tests are psychological assessment tools that require individuals to respond to a standardized set of instructions or questions. Unlike projective tests, which rely on ambiguous stimuli and open-ended responses, objective tests present clear and structured items with predetermined response options, so they cannot be interpreted qualitatively by an external reviewer. Although some projective tests do have a scoring and ranking system, objective tests almost always do, and this standardized scoring mechanism is free of rater bias – that is, free from influence or intervention on the part of the assessor.

Since objective tests are largely self-report questionnaires, they rely on a degree of honesty and self-reflection in the subject. It is also relatively easy for people to respond in a way that either portrays traits they think are desirable or skews the result to a particular outcome.

The most common form of objective test in personality psychology is the self-report measure. They typically use multiple-choice items or numbered scales, which represent a range from 1 (strongly disagree) to 5 (strongly agree) – known as a Likert scale and named after the

American social psychologist Rensis Likert. They may also use true/false statements, multiple-choice questions or forced-choice formats.

Objective tests are widely used for research, clinical assessment and screening purposes in counselling, clinical psychology, educational psychology, organizational psychology and forensic psychology. Objective tests provide standardized and quantifiable measures of personality traits, psychological symptoms, intelligence, attitudes, interests and other psychological constructs.

There is ongoing debate among psychologists and researchers regarding the validity and reliability of objective tests. Critics argue that self-report inventories may be susceptible to response biases, such as social desirability bias (answering in a way they think makes them look better) or acquiescence bias (the tendency for participants to agree with research statements), which could affect the accuracy of individuals' responses. Proponents say that objective tests can provide valuable and reliable information about individuals' psychological characteristics when designed and administered appropriately. They emphasize the importance of psychometric properties, such as reliability and validity, in evaluating the effectiveness of these tests.

The Myers-Briggs Type Indicator

The Myers-Briggs Type Indicator (MBTI) is based on Carl Jung's theory of personality types, which was further developed by Katharine Briggs and Isabel Briggs Myers into a standardized test with 16 defined types (see chapter two). A combination of the two attitudes and four functions, with the addition of perception and judgement, which were regarded as implicit in Jung's work, give these 16 different types. The MBTI has become the most widespread commercial application of Jungian theory. It has been criticized as pseudoscientific however, for its lack of statistical validity and low reliability.

The Myers-Briggs framework is made up of eight preferences which are organized into four pairs of opposites. According to the Myers-Briggs Foundation, your MBTI personality type represents your natural preferences in four important aspects of personality.

Respondents are asked the question "What do you prefer?", and scored on their responses to questions on these preference pairs:

Extraversion (E) or Introversion (I)
Opposite ways to direct and receive energy

Sensing (S) or Intuition (N)
Opposite ways to take in information

Thinking (T) or Feeling (F)
Opposite ways to decide and come to conclusions

Judging (J) or Perceiving (P)
Opposite ways to approach the outside world

Once the E-I, S-N, T-F, J-P pairs have been scored, each person is assigned a type, based on their most dominant preferences. When the letters for each of these preferences are combined, 16 distinct personality types form, consisting of different characteristics unique to that type, for example INFP, ESFJ or ISTJ. Each type has an associated description designed to give insight into how to use your natural strengths and communication styles to solve problems, manage conflict and deal with stress.

The MBTI has been adapted into many different online quizzes and personality assessments based on popular culture, and its 16 types form the basis of hundreds of other spinoff videos and articles, some of which compare each type to famous writers, actors, scientists or other celebrities. It is readily available online, for example as the 16Personalities test.

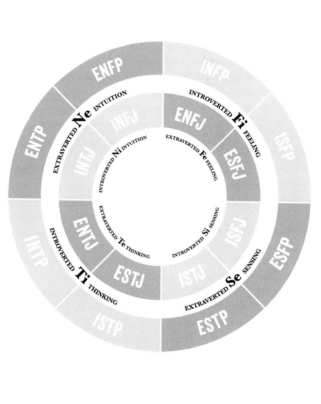

Minnesota Multiphasic Personality Inventory

The Minnesota Multiphasic Personality Inventory (MMPI) is one of the most commonly used psychological tests and is now in its third edition, MMPI-3. The test involves completing a series of questions corresponding to various scales used in the diagnosis of certain mental health conditions like schizophrenia, depression and anxiety. However, mental health professionals don't rely on the results alone when making a diagnosis. Different versions of the test are used for different people – for example the MMPI-A and MMPI-A-RF are designed for use with teenagers aged 14 to 18, while the rest of the tests are for those over 18.

Lawyers also use the MMPI as forensic evidence in criminal cases, and employers sometimes use the test in job screenings for high-risk roles, such as police officers, pilots, air-traffic controllers or nuclear power plant personnel.

The University of Minnesota first published the test by Starke R. Hathaway and J. C. McKinley in 1942 and owns the copyright. It only licenses the test to credentialled professionals, so this is not an assessment you can freely do online without the supervision of a licensed practitioner.

The test can be scored by hand or by a computer, but the results should always be interpreted by a qualified mental health professional who has had extensive training in MMPI interpretation. When the test is updated, the norms and scales used to score the test are also updated. The first three scales are Hypochondriasis, Depression and Hysteria. Each test version also contains varying content scales, clinical subscales and supplementary scales. These might be used to test the validity of the results and detect unusual patterns in the answers.

Interpreting the MMPI is a complex process that is closely protected and monitored. This is because the complex scale requires specific training to accurately interpret the results – and misinterpreting the results can lead to unnecessary distress.

Defining Terms

NORM

Statistic or set of statistics that researchers compare an individual's score against. This helps researchers determine the baseline "normal", or typical, result.

SCALE

A set of questions that measure a person's tendency towards a certain mental health condition. They can also measure aspects of mental or social functioning that don't necessarily indicate a disorder.

The Big Five and HEXACO

The Big Five personality test, also known as the Five-Factor Model (FFM), is a widely accepted framework for understanding personality traits. It categorizes personality into five dimensions: Openness to Experience, Conscientiousness, Extraversion, Agreeableness and Neuroticism (OCEAN). These dimensions encompass a range of traits, from creativity and curiosity to emotional stability and sociability.

This test is extensively used in psychology, both in research and applied settings, due to its comprehensive coverage of personality traits. Researchers use the Big Five to study various aspects of human behaviour, such as job performance, relationship dynamics and mental health outcomes. Moreover, it has practical applications in fields like personnel selection, career counselling and psychotherapy.

The Big Five's validity is supported by a substantial body of research, demonstrating its reliability in predicting behaviour across different contexts and cultures. Studies have consistently shown correlations between Big Five traits and real-world outcomes, such as job performance, academic achievement and interpersonal relationships.

However, the Big Five is not without its limitations. Critics argue that it oversimplifies the complexity of personality by reducing it to five broad dimensions, potentially overlooking unique individual differences. Additionally, some cultural variations in the interpretation of personality traits may not be fully captured by the test's universal framework.

A new model, HEXACO, was developed by Kibeom Lee and Michael Ashton, and expands upon the Big Five model with one additional trait: Honesty-Humility, which they describe as how much a person places others' interests over their own.

The Big Five remains one of the most robust and widely used personality assessments in psychology. Its versatility, reliability and cross-cultural validity make it a valuable tool for understanding human behaviour and informing practical interventions in various domains of life. Rather than assigning a yes/no value to each personality dimension, the Big Five test scores each trait along a continuum, so the results can be plotted on a five-sided shape, rather than conform to a set choice of types. Like the Big Five test, the HEXACO can be plotted, this time using the extra dimension – on a hexagon.

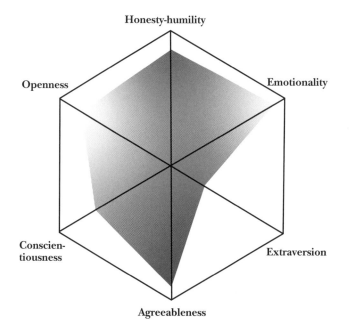

The Enneagram

The Enneagram is a personality typing system that categorizes individuals into nine distinct types, each with its own core motivations, fears and defence mechanisms. The system suggests that people develop coping strategies in response to childhood experiences, these patterns lasting throughout their lives. These types are:

- The reformer: rational, idealistic: principled, purposeful, self-controlled, perfectionistic

- The helper: caring, interpersonal type: demonstrative, generous, people-pleasing, possessive

- The achiever: success-oriented, pragmatic: adaptive, excelling, driven, image-conscious

- The individualist: sensitive, withdrawn: expressive, dramatic, self-absorbed, temperamental

- The investigator: intense, cerebral: perceptive, innovative, secretive, isolated

- The loyalist: committed, security-oriented: engaging, responsible, anxious, suspicious

- The enthusiast: busy, fun-loving: spontaneous, versatile, distractible, scattered

- The challenger: powerful, dominating: self-confident, decisive, wilful, confrontational

- The peacemaker: easy-going, self-effacing: receptive, reassuring, agreeable, complacent

Each type also has a unique path of growth and stress, with potential for integration (positive growth) and disintegration (negative behaviours). The Enneagram helps individuals recognize their core motivations and patterns of behaviour. The Enneagram supposes that having been born with a dominant type and inborn temperament, we emerge from childhood with one of the nine types dominating our personality. This inborn orientation determines how we learn to adapt to our early childhood environment.

The Enneagram of personality types is a synthesis of many ancient traditions, but the "traditional Enneagram" has its origins in the late 1960s, when the Bolivian Oscar Ichazo began teaching his methods to visiting Americans. He was allegedly inspired by Plato's Divine Forms. While dismissed as pseudoscience, other studies have shown that the test offered by the Enneagram Institute called RHETI® – Riso-Hudson Enneagram Type Indicator – has been found statistically acceptable for personality research purposes.

The Market for Personality

Personality quizzes are used in marketing for lead generation, advertising campaigns, selling data and predicting romantic matches. In the human resources field there are many online tests, personality inventories and systems to help employees and employers identify key strengths and find the best professional fit for their personality. While some tests are endorsed by psychologists, others are little more than a seductively expensive gimmick, as most of these tests aren't free, or will only allow you to take a limited version of the test for free and then offer a comprehensive report for a fee.

If you are uncertain whether a test is a good investment, try to read around the free results initially and use your common sense. You may be paying for a life-changing insight, or perhaps just for some entertainment... which is fine, too, if it's a transaction you're happy to make.

THE GOOD LIFE IS A PROCESS, NOT A STATE OF BEING. IT IS A DIRECTION, NOT A DESTINATION.

Carl Rogers, *On Becoming a Person*

Looking Further Afield

As the world becomes more connected, who has the right to define what personality is across cultures and who has the right to hold data that might predict or inform decisions about, or made based on, your personality?

In psychology, WEIRD stands for Western, Educated, Industrialized, Rich and Democratic: the demographic base of so much psychology research, especially in the twentieth century. Does personality testing work the same way in cultures outside those in which they were designed? Only by combining their outsider description (called an "etic" account) with proper description and lived experience of a behaviour or belief from within a culture (called an "emic" account), will researchers gain any useful insights or knowledge. After all, people's culture affects their behaviour outside of the bounds of any personality theory – especially if that theory hasn't accounted for the cultural difference.

WHAT LIES BEHIND US AND
WHAT LIES BEFORE US ARE
TINY MATTERS COMPARED
TO WHAT LIES WITHIN US.

Ralph Waldo Emerson

PERSONALITY DISORDERS

So far we've looked at how we describe, think about and test personality, and how each of us has a mixture of genetic and environmental factors which contribute to our personality and define its traits. For most people, personality traits and patterns of thinking are relatively stable over time, and the way we react to situations is consistent.

Sometimes, though, people react to situations and emotions in a disordered way. Patterns of behaviour or thought might become unstable or excessively rigid, and when this happens, it can be hard to adapt to a situation. Work, relationships, health and self-esteem may suffer. In this case, a person might be diagnosed with a personality disorder – something that can only be done by a mental health professional. Personality disorder diagnosis is a relatively young field with developing and new treatments.

It's generally accepted that there are ten different personality disorders, which can be grouped into three categories: suspicious, emotional and impulsive, and anxious. People can meet the diagnostic criteria for more than one disorder, which is called mixed personality disorder.

As we go through the next pages, be aware that they are not designed to make any kind of diagnosis, but to provide you with information. If you think you might be affected by any of these symptoms, please talk to your doctor.

Suspicious Personality Disorders

Suspicious personality disorders are characterized by a difficulty relating to others. People affected by a disorder in this group may be seen to be odd or eccentric. Conditions within this category are:

- Paranoid personality disorder
- Schizoid personality disorder
- Schizotypal personality disorder

Having one of these disorders, or suspecting you might have one, doesn't mean you can't or shouldn't take personality tests; the tests used by clinicians to diagnose personality disorders are not the same as the standard personality tests in the previous chapter. You should, however, make sure you get advice from a mental health professional if you need to ask questions about yourself or someone close to you who you think may be affected by a personality disorder.

PARANOID PERSONALITY DISORDER

People with this type of disorder often feel that they can't trust others, even close family or friends. They may feel they are being lied to constantly. It might be common in everyday speech to use the term "paranoid" when describing an interaction with someone, but paranoid personality disorder is diagnosed when there are specific symptoms and a pervasive pattern of distrust and suspicion which extends to the belief that someone will cause the person harm. People with paranoid personality disorder may feel easily rejected and get jealous very easily, making relationships difficult. They may also misinterpret neutral remarks as hostile or belittling, and hold grudges easily.

Treatment by a trained psychiatrist or mental health professional may take the form of cognitive behavioural therapy (CBT). If you have been diagnosed with paranoid personality disorder, your psychiatrist should rule out schizophrenia, psychosis, PTSD and mood disorders.

THE DIAGNOSIS OF PARANOID PERSONALITY DISORDER

A person can receive a diagnosis of paranoid personality disorder if they are shown to be persistently suspicious and distrustful of other people. This in turn is demonstrated if four or more of the following criteria are met, and the symptoms have begun by early adulthood:

- Without justification, they believe that others are deceiving them, hurting or otherwise exploiting them.
- They are unjustifiably preoccupied with doubts about how reliable their friends or colleagues are.
- They resist confiding in other people because they worry that information might be used against them.
- They take offence at harmless remarks and misinterpret them as having hidden hostile, demeaning or threatening meanings.
- They are prone to holding a grudge if they believe they've been insulted or injured.
- They are always ready to believe their reputation or character is under attack, and will defend or counter readily.
- They frequently have unjustified beliefs that their spouse or partner might be cheating on them.

SCHIZOID PERSONALITY DISORDER

People with this type of disorder find it hard to form social relationships and may be completely uninterested in doing so. They have difficulty relating to others in a meaningful way and prefer to be alone. The pervasive pattern of behaviour in this disorder is detachment from relationships and limited expression of emotions. They may miss social cues and show indifference to the praise or criticism of others. Symptoms begin by early adulthood and may be helped by CBT.

People with schizoid personality disorder are more likely to have a depressive disorder and may also have other personality disorders.

THE DIAGNOSIS OF SCHIZOID PERSONALITY DISORDER

A person can receive a diagnosis of schizoid personality disorder if they are shown to be detached and generally disinterested in social relationships, with a limited way of expressing emotion in interpersonal interactions. This in turn is shown by four or more of the following criteria being met, as well as the onset of symptoms by early adulthood:

- They don't express a desire to be in or enjoy close relationships, including those with family members.

- They overwhelmingly prefer to be alone.

- Having sex with another person doesn't interest them.

- They enjoy a very narrow range of or no activities.

- Apart from possibly immediate family, they lack close friends or people they can confide in.

- They seem indifferent when they are praised or criticized.

- They come across detached and cold emotionally, with a flat affect.

SCHIZOTYPAL PERSONALITY DISORDER

Like those people with schizoid personality disorder, people with this disorder are often cold, distant and introverted, and have an intense fear of intimacy and closeness, preferring not to interact with people, as this can create a pattern of intense discomfort. However, people with schizotypal personality disorder also exhibit disordered thinking, perception and ineffective communication skills. Many symptoms of schizotypal personality disorder look like schizophrenia, but are not as intense or intrusive. Treatment for schizotypal personality disorder includes antipsychotic medications, antidepressants and CBT.

Over half of people with schizotypal personality disorder have had at least one episode of major depressive disorder, and 30 to 50 per cent of them have major depressive disorder when schizotypal personality disorder is diagnosed.

THE DIAGNOSIS OF SCHIZOTYPAL PERSONALITY DISORDER

A diagnosis of schizoid personality disorder is usually made when a person is intensely uncomfortable and incapable in close relationships, combined with eccentric behaviour and perceptual or cognitive distortion. This in turn is shown by five or more of the following criteria being met, as well as the onset of symptoms by early adulthood:

- They have "ideas of reference" (thinking that everyday events hold some special significance only for or directed at them) but not "delusions of reference" (these are essentially the same but beliefs are held with even more conviction).

- They are given to magical thinking (for instance, strong belief in clairvoyant, extrasensory, telepathic powers or the paranormal).

- They report strange perceptual experiences (for instance, hearing voices calling to them).

- They use odd patterns of speech and thought (eccentric, unusual).

- Their behaviour or way they look or dress is eccentric.

- They have paranoid or suspicious thoughts.

- Their affect is incongruous or limited.

- Apart from possibly immediate family, they lack close friends or people they can confide in.

- They have social anxiety that is linked with paranoid fears and doesn't diminish with familiarity.

Emotional and Impulsive Personality Disorders

Emotional and impulsive personality disorders are grounded in a severe difficulty with managing emotions, sometimes even an inability to do so. People with these kinds of personality disorders may appear unpredictable to outsiders. Conditions within this category are:

- Antisocial personality disorder
- Borderline personality disorder
- Histrionic personality disorder
- Narcissistic personality disorder

Everybody may have certain narcissistic or antisocial tendencies from time to time, but this doesn't mean they have a personality disorder. When doctors diagnose a personality disorder, they base their diagnosis on the criteria in the *Diagnostic and Statistical Manual of Mental Disorders, Fifth Edition, Text Revision* (*DSM-5-TR*), the standard reference for psychiatric diagnosis from the American Psychiatric Association. Each disorder has various reference lists that doctors can use to compare symptoms and behaviour against.

THE ONLY NORMAL PEOPLE ARE THE ONES YOU DON'T KNOW VERY WELL.

Alfred Adler

ANTISOCIAL PERSONALITY DISORDER

Antisocial personality disorder is a mental health condition that is characterized by a pervasive pattern of disregard for consequences and for the rights of others. It is three times more common among men than women. People with this personality disorder may be impulsive, reckless, easily frustrated, aggressive or prone to violence. They may seem to show little or no remorse for their actions, and seem to justify or find reasons for acting the way they do. The disorder becomes less common in older age groups, suggesting that people do learn over time to change their behaviour. Antisocial personality disorder is difficult to treat, but psychotherapy in which people are rewarded for positive behavioural change, and in some cases certain medications, may help reduce aggressive and impulsive behaviour.

People are not diagnosed with antisocial personality disorder until they are 18 or over, but this diagnosis relies on evidence that a conduct disorder has been present before they reach 15 years of age.

THE DIAGNOSIS OF ANTISOCIAL PERSONALITY DISORDER

A person can be diagnosed with antisocial personality disorder if they are shown to hold a persistent disregard for other people's rights. This in turn is demonstrated by three or more of the following criteria being met.

- They demonstrate disregard for the law and frequently get or risk getting arrested.

- They frequently lie, use an alias, con and deceive for pleasure or personal gain.

- They are impulsive in their actions and don't plan ahead.

- They are often in physical fights and are easy to provoke, aggressive and may assault others.

- They have a disregard for their own safety and that of others.

- Their actions are consistently irresponsible – for instance, not paying bills, or suddenly quitting a job with no notice or prospects.

- They do not feel guilty or remorseful about hurting or mistreating other people, but rather are indifferent to or try to rationalize the behaviour.

BORDERLINE PERSONALITY DISORDER

People living with borderline personality disorder (BPD) experience strong mood swings and pervasive patterns of unstable self-image, relationships and behaviour. It is common for those with BPD to fear rejection and abandonment, and to hate being alone. They may either disassociate or become suicidal. They may have trouble controlling anger, and be constantly changing their hair and appearance, as well as careers, friends, goals and location. Some people with BPD self-harm, binge eat or drive dangerously with little care for their safety. They may sabotage themselves just before reaching a goal, for instance, dropping out of school just before final exams.

Treatment includes group psychotherapy and dialectical behavioural therapy, as well as sometimes antidepressants or mood stabilizing medications.

THE DIAGNOSIS OF BORDERLINE PERSONALITY DISORDER

A person can be diagnosed with BPD if they demonstrate a persistent pattern of pronounced impulsivity and emotional dysregulation. This in turn is demonstrated by five or more of the following criteria being met, as well as the onset of symptoms by early adulthood (symptoms may begin in adolescence):

- They make desperate efforts to avoid either real or perceived abandonment.

- Their relationships are intense and unstable, and they swing between idealizing and devaluing the other person.

- Their sense of self or self-image is unstable.

- They are impulsive in at least two areas that could cause them harm (like dangerous driving, binge eating or unsafe sex).

- They threaten or attempt suicide, self-harm or suicidal gestures.

- Their mood changes rapidly and is usually only stable for hours at a time (rarely for more than a few days).

- They persistently experience feeling empty.

- They have problems controlling their anger, which at times is inappropriately intense.

- They experience paranoid thoughts (temporary) or stress-triggered severe dissociative symptoms.

HISTRIONIC PERSONALITY DISORDER

People with histrionic personality disorder experience discomfort if they are not the centre of attention and will take radical steps to ensure that they are. This may include dressing or behaving inappropriately, being provocative or submissive, and changing their physical appearance to appear more attractive. They may seem shallow to others, as they can turn emotions on and off quickly, and may try to manipulate a partner, while at the same time being quite dependent and easily influenced. Symptoms begin by early adulthood.

People with histrionic personality disorder may also have another disorder such as borderline, antisocial or narcissistic disorder, or somatic symptom disorder, which is when chronic physical symptoms accompany worry and stress, even when there is no physical disorder.

THE DIAGNOSIS OF HISTRIONIC PERSONALITY DISORDER

A person can be diagnosed with histrionic personality disorder if they demonstrate a persistent pattern of attention seeking and excessive emotionality. This in turn is shown by five or more of the following criteria being met, as well as the onset of symptoms by early adulthood.

- They dislike not being the focus of attention and feel discomfort.

- They interact with other people in a way that is inappropriately sexual.

- Their face shows a shallow, rapidly changing expression.

- They draw attention to themselves via physical appearance.

- They talk in a way that is vague and impressionistic.

- They use an exaggerated way to express emotion, self-dramatizing and being theatrical.

- They are highly suggestible (other people or situations easily sway them).

- They interpret relationships as being more intimate than they really are.

NARCISSISTIC PERSONALITY DISORDER

Narcissistic personality disorder is a mental health condition that is characterized by a pervasive pattern of feeling superior (grandiosity), needing admiration and lacking empathy. Beginning by early adulthood, people with narcissistic personality disorder tend to have an exaggerated sense of their own talents and importance and will exploit and devalue others, seek out sources of admiration and try to become part of exclusive, important or superior groups or institutions. They often think they deserve special privileges or allowances, but withdraw if criticism is levelled at them.

One theory on narcissism is that the problem starts early, when parents or caregivers don't enable the child to develop a stable sense of self.

People with this disorder often also have depression or another personality disorder, or problems with substance abuse or anorexia nervosa. Treatment for narcissistic personality disorder may include psychodynamic talking therapy or CBT.

THE DIAGNOSIS OF NARCISSISTIC PERSONALITY DISORDER

A person can be diagnosed with narcissistic personality disorder if they demonstrate a persistent pattern of grandiosity. They lack empathy and have a constant need to be admired. This in turn is shown by five or more of the following criteria being met, as well as the onset of symptoms by early adulthood:

- They demonstrate grandiosity, which is an exaggerated and baseless sense of their own importance and talents.

- They are preoccupied with fantasies of great achievements, power, influence, intelligence, beauty or perfect love.

- They hold the belief that they are unique, special and should socialize only with people of the highest calibre.

- They need to be admired without conditions.

- They use exploitation of others to get ahead.

- They have a lack of empathy.

- They feel envious of others and believe that others envy them.

- They are haughty and arrogant.

Anxious Personality Disorders

These are marked by a level of anxiety that is inhibiting everyday life and relationships.

Conditions within this category are:

- Avoidant personality disorder
- Dependent personality disorder
- Obsessive-compulsive personality disorder

We've covered the three anxious personality disorders here, along with the other seven which make up this chapter. Some people meet certain of the criteria for some of these disorders, but not fully enough to meet the clinical criteria for diagnosis of a particular named disorder. It is possible, if you have enough personality disorder traits, to receive a diagnosis of personality disorder not otherwise specified (PD-NOS).

While anxious personality disorders are characterized by a level of anxiety that makes it difficult to live a normal life, you can still have anxiety symptoms or a diagnosis of anxiety without having a personality disorder.

AVOIDANT PERSONALITY DISORDER

Avoidant personality disorder is characterized by avoiding social situations that involve risk of rejection, criticism or humiliation. This might mean avoiding specific social interactions, interpersonal contact or gatherings which might trigger the fear of seeming socially inept or inadequate compared to everybody else. Sufferers go out of their way to avoid exposure at work and school, and often have the idea that they will be "found out" and rejected, ridiculed or shamed. This can result in feelings of social exclusion and loneliness, and a reluctance to try new activities that involve other people. They may crave affection and belonging, but not be able to achieve it, and as a result feel hopeless.

Avoidance in social situations has been observed in very young children, who may be born with an innate social anxiety and reserved nature. Rejection and marginalization during early childhood may also fuel avoidant personality disorder.

Another anxiety disorder such as panic disorder or social phobia, as well as a depressive disorder or obsessive-compulsive disorder, may also be present in the sufferer. Treatment may include CBT and psychodynamic therapy, as well as some anti-anxiety or antidepressant medication prescribed by a doctor.

THE DIAGNOSIS OF AVOIDANT PERSONALITY DISORDER

A person can be diagnosed with avoidant personality disorder if they demonstrate a persistent pattern of avoiding social contact and they feel inadequate. They are also hypersensitive to rejection and criticism. This in turn is shown by four or more of the following criteria being met, as well as the onset of symptoms by early adulthood:

- They avoid any face-to-face contact at work for fear of criticism, rejection or disapproval.

- They are not willing to get involved with others until they are sure they will be liked.

- They exhibit reserve in close relationships for fear of being humiliated or ridiculed.

- They are preoccupied with being rejected or criticized in a social environment.

- They are inhibited when in a social situation because of feelings of inadequacy.

- They self-identify as socially incompetent, inferior to others or unappealing.

- They are slow or reluctant to take a risk or participate in new activities for fear of being embarrassed.

DEPENDENT PERSONALITY DISORDER

Those with dependent personality disorder typically put their own needs after people around them, as a strategy to be taken care of themselves. They avoid looking after themselves and have a pervasive need to be looked after by another person, which may lead to them giving up their independence and becoming submissive. Sufferers lack in confidence and self-efficacy, and may tolerate abuse in order to get the attention and care they seek. They also struggle with decision-making, initiating projects alone and expressing disagreement in fear of being judged or abandoned. These symptoms will start by early adulthood.

Treatment may include psychodynamic therapy and CBT, focusing on fears of independence and problems of self-assertiveness.

THE DIAGNOSIS OF DEPENDENT PERSONALITY DISORDER

A person can be diagnosed with dependent personality disorder if they demonstrate a persistent, excessive need to be taken care of, which results in clingy, submissive behaviour and constant fear of being apart. This in turn is shown by five or more of the following criteria being met, as well as the onset of symptoms by early adulthood:

- They find it difficult to make everyday decisions unless they elicit a great deal of advice and reassurance from other people.

- They need others to take responsibility for important aspects of their life.

- They find it difficult to express disagreement with others because they are scared of losing support or approval.

- They find it difficult to start a project alone, because they don't feel confident about their abilities and/or judgement (rather than being lacking in energy or motivation).

- They are prepared to go to great lengths (e.g., do unpleasant tasks) in order to get support from other people.

- They experience feelings of discomfort or helplessness when they are alone, because they fear they are incapable of looking after themselves.

- After the end of a close relationship they are keen to establish a new one to find someone who will provide care and support.

- They fear being left to take care of themselves and will worry constantly about it.

OBSESSIVE-COMPULSIVE PERSONALITY DISORDER

Obsessive-compulsive personality disorder (OCPD) is one of the most common personality disorders, occurring in 4–8 per cent of people in the United States. It is more common among men. It is not the same as obsessive-compulsive disorder (OCD) in which the sufferer experiences their thoughts as a problem, so much so that they'll perform actions (compulsions) out of fear that something bad will happen. People living with OCPD act with the personal conviction that how they do things is how things should be done. Usually, they are not aware of the negative impact their perfectionism has on coworkers, and they tend to neglect their social life in favour of work.

Certain traits that run in families like compulsivity, a limited range of emotion and perfectionism, are thought to contribute to this disorder. The disorder emerges by early adulthood.

Treatment may include psychodynamic therapy and CBT.

THE DIAGNOSIS OF OBSESSIVE-COMPULSIVE PERSONALITY DISORDER

A person can be diagnosed with OCPD if they are preoccupied with order and self-control, as well as perfectionism and control of others. This in turn is shown by four or more of the following criteria being met, as well as the onset of symptoms by early adulthood:

- They immerse themselves in rules, schedules, organizing lists and detailed plans.

- They strive so much for perfection that it interferes with completion of the task.

- They devote themselves to work and being productive (though not because they need the money) resulting in friends and leisure activity being forgotten.

- They show excessive inflexibility, are extremely conscientiousness, fastidious and have fixed ethical and moral issues and values.

- They hold on to worn out or worthless belongings, even those without sentimental value.

- They refuse or are reluctant to work with others or delegate tasks, unless things are done exactly the way they want.

- They are miserly, don't spend on themselves and see money as proofing against future disasters.

- They are stubborn and rigid.

Conclusion

Personality is such a mysterious vessel. We all have one, but none are the same. Humans have been trying to figure out what personality is for millennia. Do you think we're any closer today?

It may be comforting to think that Hippocrates was pondering the same questions as you a couple of thousand years ago. Humans have always described ourselves and each other, always written down our fears and foibles, to leave an impression for future generations so they'll know what life was like for us.

This little book has guided you through just a few of the ideas, theories, controversies, inspired discoveries and solid research that makes up the history and practice of personality psychology. We looked at ancient beliefs via the relatively modern interpretation of Freud and Jung, and those who came after, pushing and continuing to probe the boundaries of understanding, establishing new paradigms, doing real science and sometimes pseudoscience, all in the name of widening the net of understanding.

Trends in psychology come and go, as do trends in any other area of life. Together we've gained a small insight into fields like behaviourism, biological theories of psychology, personality testing and the ethics and practice of actual experiments. We've touched on Bobo dolls, on neural pathways and the unconscious, on how psychiatrists diagnose and treat personality disorders, how to test your personality and on whether all this is down to who we are at birth, or how we live.

It's impossible in a small volume to do justice to all the thinkers we've glimpsed, who have spent thousands of hours doing tedious legwork, writing papers, giving speeches and teaching. There should be more acknowledgement of the diversity of research and knowledge across the globe, and better understanding of new ways to interpret personality. But, hopefully, this book has given you a taste for new adventures in personality psychology and piqued your curiosity to discover more for yourself. Many of the personality tests have online versions you can try out and there are myriad free resources available online to take you further on your journey into the fascinating territory of personality psychology.

Resources

WEBSITES

American Psychological Association: apa.org

PracticalPie: practicalpie.com

Coursera: coursera.org/learn/introduction-psychology

Verywell Mind: verywellmind.com/psychology-4157187

The Society for Personality and Social Psychology: spsp.org/about/what-socialpersonality-psychology

MSD Manual: msdmanuals.com/home/quick-facts-mental-health-disorders/personality-disorders

Nathan Hudson: nathanwhudson.com/research

Rorschach.org: rorschach.org

Myers & Briggs Foundation: myersbriggs.org

The Enneagram Institute: enneagraminstitute.com

16Personalities: 16personalities.com

BOOKS

Alter, Adam (2014), *Drunk Tank Pink*

Buss, David (ed.) (2015), *The Handbook of Evolutionary Psychology, Volume 1: Foundation*

Cain, Susan (2013), *Quiet: The Power of Introverts in a World That Can't Stop Talking*

Corr, Philip J. and Matthews, Gerald (ed.) (2009), *The Cambridge Handbook of Personality Psychology*

Dawkins, Richard (2019), *The Selfish Gene*

Schultz, D. P. and Schultz, S. E. (2017), *Theories of Personality (Eleventh edition)*

Skinner, B. F. (1965), *Science and Human Behavior*

The Little Book of Psychology:
An Introduction to the Key Psychologists
and Theories You Need to Know

Emily Ralls & Caroline Riggs

Paperback • ISBN: 978-1-78685-807-8

If you want to know your Freud from your Jung and your
Milgram from your Maslow, this approachable little book
will take you on a whirlwind tour of the key thinkers,
themes and theories you need to know to understand how
the study of mind and behaviour has sculpted the world
we live in and the way we think today.

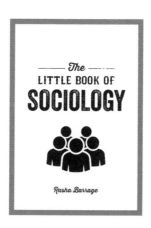

The Little Book of Sociology:
A Pocket Guide to the Study of Society

Rasha Barrage

Paperback • ISBN: 978-1-80007-718-8

If you've always wanted to know how societies function – and why sometimes they don't – this beginner's guide to sociology has got the essential theories and thinkers covered. Perfect for newcomers, or anyone seeking a concise breakdown of the subject, *The Little Book of Sociology* takes all the big ideas and makes them crystal clear.

Have you enjoyed this book? If so, find us on Facebook at **SUMMERSDALE PUBLISHERS**, on Twitter/X at **@SUMMERSDALE** and on Instagram and TikTok at **@SUMMERSDALEBOOKS** and get in touch. We'd love to hear from you!

WWW.SUMMERSDALE.COM